the palace of VERSAILLES

Author: Antony Mason

Copyright © *ticktock* Entertainment Ltd 2005
First published in Great Britain in 2005 by *ticktock* Media Ltd.,
Unit 2, Orchard Business Centre, North Farm Road, Tunbridge Wells, Kent, TN2 3XF
We would like to thank: Susan Barraclough, Elizabeth Wiggans and Jenni Rainford for their help with
this book.
ISBN 1 86007 598 3 PB
Printed in China
A CIP catalogue record for this book is available from the British Library.

Contents

Introduction

The magnificent Palace of Versailles is one of the most popular tourist destinations in France – and it is easy to understand why. Vast, grand and filled with treasures, Versailles was Louis XIV's public showcase, attended by 7,000 courtiers. From 1682 to 1789, the palace was the principal home to the French royal family. Later, Versailles continued to play a significant role in politics. Today, the palace and gardens attract nine million visitors every year.

FIT FOR A KING

When Louis XIV came to the throne in 1643, France was one of the world's most prosperous and powerful states in Europe. It had by far the largest population in Europe – about 21 million people, while Spain had 7 million and the British Isles had 5.5 million. When the king assumed government he wanted a palace that reflected his power. The site he chose was an old royal hunting lodge, 16 kilometres to the southwest of Paris, his capital city. Here, there was plenty of space to build on a huge scale, and to create a grand garden filled with fountains, with a park attached for hunting.

Louis XIV was a king who loved to be on display to his public. With the Palace of Versailles, he aimed to build a showcase of the most lavish proportions.

4

BUILDING THE PERFECT PALACE

Louis XIV's palace was the great wonder of its day. It was built to the highest standards, and no money was spared on the most talented architects and craftsmen that France had to offer. Work continued during the reigns of Louis XIV's successors – Louis XV (reigned 1715–74) and Louis XVI (reigned 1774–93) – who developed the area around the other, more private, palaces in the grounds, the 'Grand Trianon' and the 'Petit Trianon'.

RESTORATION

During the 17th and 18th centuries, Versailles (and those who inhabited it) symbolised an extravagance that was at odds with the people of France, many of whom were going hungry. This resentment contributed to the French Revolution of 1789, which later led to the overthrow of the monarchy. Versailles was saved from new turmoil and used as a palace once more by Napoleon from 1810 to 1814, and then as a museum and public building from the 1830s. Treaties were signed at Versailles at the end of the Franco-Prussian War in 1871, and after World War I in 1919.

The magnificent Hall of Mirrors is one of the palace's greatest treasures. The Treaty of Versailles was signed here in 1919 officially ending World War I.

For decades, the palace has remained a rather soulless labyrinth of grand rooms. In recent years, however, a huge restoration project has been under way, and many items of furniture that once belonged to the palace have been returned. Each phase of restoration helps to revive the extraordinary sense of luxury, wealth and power that Versailles once had, and makes it easier to picture how it might have been in the glorious days of Louis XIV.

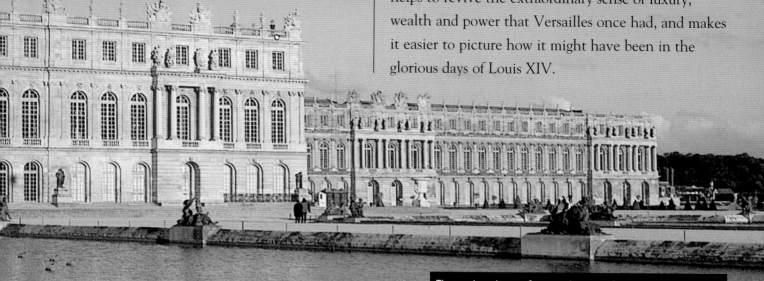

The ponds and water features play a significant role in the style and character of Versailles. This is a view of the palace from the south.

5

CHAPTER 1

How it was built

Work began on the new palace of Versailles in 1661 and took over 50 years to complete. Louis XIV wanted to create the grandest palace in Europe, adorned with the most spectacular gardens, lakes and fountains. The finest architects and designers oversaw a staggering 36,000 workmen. In the 18th century, additional buildings were added to the grand site – for housing courtiers and, more scandalously, the royal mistresses.

MODEST BEGINNINGS

In 1623, King Louis XIII built an attractive château at Versailles which became his royal hunting lodge. After his death, his son and the new king, Louis XIV, decided to make Versailles the site of his main palace. He was inspired by the palace of his ex-Finance Minister, Nicolas Fouquet, so much so that he employed the same architect, Louis Le Vau.

The transformation at Versailles took place in three phases. In the first phase (from 1661), changes were made to the Grand

Major changes took place at Versailles in the late 17th century. Phase one included creating a massive canal to drain the swampy land and make way for the gardens (above left); Phase two (above) involved building and decorating the State Apartments.

Tales & customs – THE SUN KING

Louis XIV danced in a ballet called 'The Night' when he was 15 years old. Wearing a golden mask, he performed the central role of the Sun. Because of the splendours of his court, and the success of his early reign, he became popularly known as the 'Sun King'. He also liked to think of himself as Apollo, the Greek and Roman god of the sun. There are references to the sun and Apollo all over Versailles. In addition, Versailles itself was built to face the sun.

Courtyard and to the front of the building. Then, in 1667, the Grand Canal was drained to create a park. In the second phase, Le Vau created a much grander exterior. The style was 'neoclassical' – inspired by the architecture of Classical Greece and Rome, as developed by the Italian Renaissance. The western façade was redesigned to create an impressive frontage overlooking the terraced gardens. Behind the façade, on the first floor, a series of grand new state apartments was also built. Jules Hardouin-Mansart began the third phase of building in 1678, and gave the exterior of the palace the shape it has today. Mansart designed the North and South Wings as well as many major buildings at Versailles, including the Stables and Grand Lodgings.

ELABORATE DECORATION

Mansart designed Versailles' most famous room, the magnificent Hall of Mirrors, which was finished in 1684. At 73 metres long, it occupies almost all of the western façade of the main palace building. It is lined by 17 large mirrors on one side, which face onto 17 windows. The ornately carved plaster and sculptures are covered in gold, and chandeliers hang from the ceiling.

When Louis XIV moved into the palace on May 6, 1682, it was not finished. The chapel, for instance, designed by Robert de Cotte, was not completed until 1710, five years before the end of Louis XIV's long reign. The area around the palace was cut into huge terraces decorated with ponds and formal gardens. Large fountains formed

This 17th century print by Bonnart shows a French stonemason of the period in uniform carrying the tools of his trade. Many like him would have been employed to work on the palace.

part of this design, adorned with sculptures. Beyond these gardens lay the canals and the royal hunting forest, which was ten times the size of the park today.

WATER TROUBLES

There are over 200 kilometres of water channels, aqueducts, ditches and pipes at Versailles. Much of the system is underground, in stone-lined tunnels. The huge capacity is necessary as Versailles' 50 fountains use 3,600 cubic metres of water an hour. Versailles' water was originally supplied from the River Seine, just 12 kilometres away. The trouble

The aqueduct at Marly that stored and transported water to Versailles was proclaimed as one of the great wonders of Louis XIV's day.

was that the water had to travel uphill to a height of 16 metres in order to reach Versailles. This was achieved by the construction of a huge pump at Louveciennes: 14 huge waterwheels operating 221 pumps, which pushed the water up the hill to reservoirs near Marly. Built over a period of 30 years from 1681, the 'Marly Machine' was considered to be one of the great wonders of the world in Louis XIV's day, although even this could provide only enough water to run all the Versailles

fountains for three hours. Various schemes were hatched but none were completely successful until much later. Louis XIV liked to think he was capable of solving any technical problem and yet the problem of supplying water to Versailles bugged him for the rest of his life.

WIVES, MISTRESSES AND CULTURE

In 1670, Louis XIV built a palace for his mistress, Madame de Montespan, in the grounds of

Tales & customs – AN OPPORTUNITY MISSED

The failure to supply Versailles' fountains with adequate water has been the source of regret for centuries: '... it is an even greater shame that Louis XIV, by force of necessity, shocked by those calls for economy, which are so often the downfall of the grandest plans, ran out of patience; France would otherwise have possessed today the greatest monument on Earth.' – François-René de Chateaubriand, French writer, 1841.

This 18th-century painting shows the Queen's Village, near the Petit Trianon. Louis XVI's wife Marie-Antoinette was perceived as haughty, snobbish and extravagant by the people of France. However, she found peasant life so appealing that she had a mock village built, where her courtiers dressed up in country attire – a common fashion among the European aristocracy at the time.

Versailles, clearing a village called Trianon to make room for it. This palace was decorated with blue and white Chinese porcelain – so it was called the 'Trianon de Porcelaine'. After the death of the Queen in 1683, he married his mistress Madame de Maintenon. For her, he demolished the Trianon de Porcelaine, and in 1687 replaced it with a building faced with marble, called the 'Trianon de Marbre'. A vigorous spell of building came later in the 1760s, under the direction of Louis XV's former mistress, the great intellectual and friend of the Arts, Madame de Pompadour. Part of the exterior of the main palace was rebuilt and the magnificent Opera House was added to the North Wing in 1770. The King also built an intimate palace for Madame de Pompadour called the 'Petit Trianon'. The larger Trianon de Marbre now became known as the 'Grand Trianon'.

As country life was fashionable among the aristocracy, Louis XVI's wife, Marie Antoinette, liked to get her courtiers and ladies-in-waiting to dress as farming folk and carry out country activities in a fake rural village built nearby.

RESCUED FOR THE NATION

After the French Revolution, Napoleon Bonaparte redecorated the Grand Trianon in the new 'Empire Style' for Empress Marie Louise in 1810. He also completed the North Wing of the main palace, which had never been finished.

After the overthrow of the Bourbon monarchy in 1830, King Louis-Philippe converted the two wings into a Museum of French History, demolishing many of the apartments of the princes and courtiers to make room for it. Some changes have since been made – but what we see today has essentially remained the same for over 150 years.

Much of the Grand Trianon is decorated with rose-pink marble, such as these columns that flank a chequered walkway.

CHAPTER 2

Versailles through history

Versailles is famously known as the place where Louis XIV conducted his extraordinary public life. It also served as a stage for Louis XV's famous mistress, Madame de Pompadour, and as a playground for the frivolous queen, Marie Antoinette. But Versailles is also remembered as the place where the peace treaty was signed after World War I – a treaty that was so one-sided that some see it as one of the causes of World War II.

This ornately decorated spear was carried by the guards of Louis XIV.

RISE OF THE SUN KING

Louis XIV was the son of Louis XIII and Anne of Austria. When Louis XIII died in 1643, Louis XIV was just five years old, so while he remained a minor, his mother ruled as Regent, assisted by her chief minister, Cardinal Jules Mazarin. This was a troubled period for Europe, which was devastated by the Thirty Years' War (1618–48), a late consequence of the Reformation. At the end of the war, France emerged as the strongest power in Europe, but heavy taxes caused the people to revolt in the civil war called the Fronde (1648–52). Mazarin taught the young Louis XIV how to conduct wars and run the country, and instilled in him the concept of absolute power and the 'divine right of kings' – the belief that he had been chosen by God to rule.

When Mazarin died in 1661, Louis XIV announced that he would rule in his own right. He was assisted by a very able new chief minister, Jean-Baptiste Colbert (1619–83). Colbert reformed the tax system, encouraged trade and helped to develop industry. As a result, France grew wealthy – and so too did Louis XIV. It was now that Louis XIV began his grand building projects, first at the royal palaces in Paris, and then Versailles. These first 20 years were Louis XIV's finest. The court moved to Versailles in 1682.

This statue depicts Louis XIV dressed as a Roman emperor crushing a rebel of the Fronde revolt.

Time line		
1623	Louis XIII builds a hunting lodge at Versailles.	
1661	Work begins on the transformation of Versailles under Louis XV.	
1664	The royal menagerie is moved to Versailles.	
1667	Work begins on the Grand Canal at Versailles (completed in 1679).	
1668	Work begins on the new palace of Versailles.	
1670	Louis XIV builds the Trianon de Porcelaine for Madame de Montespan.	
1682	The royal court and parts of the aristocracy take up residence at Versailles.	

MILITARY PRIDE AND RELIGIOUS CONFLICT

War was an essential part of any great king's role, and he was flattered by his generals that he was good at it. Louis XIV liked to review the army at parades and took credit for victories. Most of his wars were connected to claims of inheritance from the Habsburgs, the ruling family of Austria, Hungary and Spain. Louis was a Bourbon, the family that had ruled France since 1589; but both his mother and his wife were Habsburgs.

Like much of Europe, France had been torn apart by religious conflict in the 16th century, as Catholics

Louis XIV was anything but a private man. In the above illustration, he is receiving visitors from the alcove of his chambers at Versailles.

fought with Huguenots (Protestants) in the Wars of Religion (1562–98). Some peace was achieved by the Edict of Nantes of 1598, which allowed freedom of worship to the Protestants. But Louis XIV, for reasons of his foreign policy and to better control his country, wanted France to be Catholic. In 1685 he withdrew the Edict of Nantes. As a result some 400,000 Huguenots emigrated abroad, most of them members of France's professional and intellectual élite.

France had been developing settlements in Canada since 1604, claiming the land as 'New France'. In 1663, Louis took control over the territories, and settlers from France began to arrive in large numbers. French explorers meanwhile headed south and carved out a vast territory for France, which in 1682 was named after Louis XIV: Louisiana. This was far larger than the modern state of Louisiana.

A QUIETER SANCTUARY

Louis XIV died in 1715, outliving his son and one of his two grandsons. As his other grandson became king of Spain, France was ruled by his brother, the Duc

1683	Queen Marie-Thérèse dies at Versailles. Louis marries his mistress, Madame de Maintenon.
1687	Louis XIV builds the Trianon de Marbre (Grand Trianon) for Madame de Maintenon.
1715	Louis XIV dies at Versailles, aged 77.

The Palace of Versailles

The Duc d'Orléans ruled France as Regent until Louis XV was old enough to rule France in his own right. In this 18th century painting, the young Louis receives a school lesson from one of his teachers.

d'Orléans, until Louis XV (the great-grandson of Louis XIV) was old enough to formally take the throne in 1723. Louis XV was a much less publicly visible king than Louis XIV, which meant that Versailles became a much quieter place than in earlier times – with much less ceremony and public entertainment. Unlike his predecessor, Louis XV preferred to retreat to the privacy of the Grand Trianon to dine with friends. The old royal court of law called 'the parlements' were gatherings of the nobility, who had historically tussled with the king. Louis XIV had ended up suppressing them; however, the Duc d'Orléans restored them again in 1718. They then became the focus of opposition to the king in the late 18th century. Towards the end of Louis XV's reign the parlement of Paris was once more suppressed, and Louis assumed power as absolute monarch.

THE SEVEN YEARS WAR

Wars still raged throughout Europe over who should succeed whom. Louis XV's gifted chief minister, Cardinal Fleury, managed to keep France out of the War of Austrian Succession (1740–48), but unfortunately France did become involved in the highly complex Seven Years

Time line

1715–22 Following the death of Louis XIV, the court abandons Versailles and moves to Paris.

1723 Louis XV succeeds the throne upon the death of the Duc d'Orleans.

1725 Louis XV marries the Polish princess Marie Leszczynska.

1757 Robert Damiens attacks and wounds the king with a penknife at Versailles. He is condemned to death, tortured with red-hot pincers and boiling oil, and torn to pieces.

1763–68 The Petit Trianon is built for Madame de Pompadour, but she dies before it can be put to use.

Scientists were making progress in many areas – such as physics, medicine and astronomy – by applying careful methods of reason, observation, theory and experiment. A similar approach was taken to philosophy and political thought, concerning such ideas as personal freedom, equality and democracy. This movement was called the 'Enlightenment'. In France, it was led by a group of thinkers and scientists known as the 'philosophes'. They had close contact with the court at Versailles; Madame de Pompadour actively encouraged the 'philosophes' to compile the great book of the Enlightenment, the *Encyclopédie*. One of its contributors was the writer Voltaire, who described Versailles as 'a masterpiece of bad taste and magnificence'.

By the end of Louis XV's reign, France was virtually bankrupt. There were numerous reasons, including the costs of war, the loss of overseas territories, and royal extravagance. Although France's finances recovered a little in the final years of his reign, when he died he left a debt of 4 billion livres (about UK£7.5 billion in modern money).

CHOOSING SIDES AND GOING IT ALONE

In 1775, the people of 13 colonies of North America began a rebellion against their British rulers, and the following year issued their famous 'Declaration of Independence'. The result was the American War of Independence. One contributor to the Declaration of Independence was the American politician and inventor Benjamin

War (1756–63). Although fought mainly in central Europe, British and French interests clashed due to their overseas possessions. As a result, France lost control of Canada and Louisiana, as well as parts of India. France, once the proud owner of valuable overseas territories, lost much wealth and prestige.

THE ENLIGHTENMENT

The 18th century was a period of scientific discovery and invention.

1768 Queen Marie dies at Versailles.

1770 The future Louis XVI marries Marie Antoinette in a spectacular celebration at Versailles; the Opera House, designed by Jacques-Ange Gabriel, is completed for the occasion.

1774 Louis XV dies at Versailles, aged 64.

The Palace of Versailles

Franklin, who became the American ambassador to Versailles. He helped to persuade France to support the Americans against Britain with troops, money and naval ships. After the last British surrender in 1781, Franklin and others negotiated for peace; in the resulting Paris Peace Treaty, signed in 1783, Britain recognised American independence.

In 1788, the government of France became bankrupt. This was caused by political conflicts and because the huge expense of funding wars had caused massive debts. Meanwhile, the tax system – needed to raise funds – was in chaos. All the while the royal court continued to spend lavishly, which only incited resentment amongst the people. A harvest failure added to poor people's anger, as they now faced rises in

This painting shows a group of counter-revolutionaries singing during the 1789 French Revolution. The Revolution was an uprising of the people against their extravagant monarchy.

the price of bread. The State Generals were summoned to Versailles in 1789. The Commoners, however, who formed a majority, gathered at the royal tennis court in the town of Versailles on June 20. They swore that they would not disband until their demands were met by Louis XVI. On June 17th, the State Generals declared themselves the National Assembly.

REVOLUTION

The people of Paris were furious about the concentration of troops in the capital and the general economic situation. On July 14, 1789, they attacked an old prison called the Bastille – a symbol of royal oppression. This has later been described as the start of the French Revolution.

On October 5, 1789 craftsmen from Paris and their wives marched on Versailles, demanding bread, and for the royal court to return to Paris where they could be more closely watched by the citizenry. The following day rioters broke into the palace and massacred the guards defending the Queen's Suite. Only the help of the Marquis de Lafayette prevented the massacre of the royal family. After having tried to leave the country, Louis XVI and Marie Antoinette were eventually

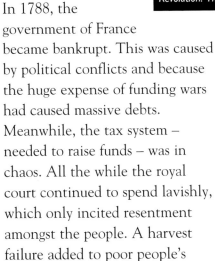

Time line

1774   Louis XVI is crowned king of France.

1775–84
       Marie Antoinette builds the Hameau de la Reine.

1788   France becomes bankrupt.

1789   The French Revolution forces Louis XVI and his family to leave Versailles for Paris. The people attack the Bastille.

1792   Versailles is stripped of many of its contents. France is declared a Republic. France declares war against Austria and Prussia. This is the start of the French Revolutionary Wars.

1793   Louis XVI is executed by guillotine in January; Marie Antoinette is executed in October.

executed for treason in 1793. In 1792, the National Convention declared France to be a Republic – a country ruled by the people. Meanwhile, the new government in Paris began to fear that French opponents of the Revolution, who had fled abroad, would persuade foreign enemies to attack. In April 1792, war was declared against Austria and Prussia. This was the start of the French Revolutionary Wars. The Revolution profoundly transformed French society by making all citizens equal, limiting the influence of religion on public life, liberating the economy and administrative reforms – such as the introduction of the metric system – all over France. The changes were mostly to the

This portrait shows Louis XVI's frivolous queen Marie Antoinette in hunting attire.

advantage of the middle classes. Attacks on the Revolution from the outside and inside the Republic caused its leader Maximilien Robespierre to use terror to control the situation, resulting in the execution of about 35,000 people. By now France was in a state of turmoil. But Robespierre was eventually overthrown and executed in 1794, and power was handed over to a new government – this marked the start of a more orderly and peaceful period.

This 18th century cartoon illustrates October 5, 1789, when a crowd consisting mainly of women stormed the palace of Versailles, calling for food and for the royal family to return to Paris.

1793   Robespierre leads the Reign of Terror. He is eventually overthrown and executed in 1794.

1795   The Dauphin (Crown Prince) dies in mysterious circumstances.

1795–99
    The Directory results in a period of stagnation in revolutionary France.

AN EMPEROR OR A KING?

Napoleon Bonaparte was just 30 years old when he seized control of France. A successful general in the Revolutionary Wars, he now launched a series of wars across

The Palace of Versailles

Europe, called the Napoleonic Wars. Napoleon restored Versailles and redecorated the Grand Trianon in the new 'Empire Style'. This style was neoclassical and intended to symbolise the harmony of all things under Napoleon's leadership. The rise of Napoleon gave Europe 25 years of turmoil and war, but also an important period of modernisation, ending with his final defeat in 1815.

The victorious Allies believed the best way to restore order to France was to reinstate the monarchy of the Bourbons. So, Louis XVIII was placed on the throne. Under the new king, the North Wing at Versailles was completed. Louis was succeeded by his brother Charles X. His tyrannical regime was overthrown by the Revolution of 1830 and he was replaced by the Duc d'Orléans,

Louis-Philippe. His constitutional monarchy led to a financial crisis and provoked a revolution in 1848, forcing him to abdicate.

This neoclassical painting shows Napoleon Bonaparte on horseback. Napoleon did a great deal to restore Versailles, such as renovating the Grand Trianon.

This swept the monarchy aside for a second time. France became a republic once more.

In 1852, a nephew of Napoleon and elected president organised a coup against the republic and took the title of Emperor Napoleon III. In 1870, a dispute with Prussia led to war, and France was rapidly overrun. Versailles became the headquarters of the Prussian army in 1870, the residence of the King of Prussia and a hospital. In 1871, a peace treaty was signed at Versailles. At the same time, the German states unified as one nation-state, and William I of Prussia was proclaimed German Emperor in the Hall of Mirrors. The Third Republic was formed during the Franco-Prussian War. The Opera House of Versailles became the setting for meetings of the National Assembly, then in 1875 a Congressional Chamber was built in the South Wing.

Time line

1810	Empress Marie-Louise, second wife of Napoleon, takes up residence in the Grand Trianon.	
1820	Building work on the North Wing is completed.	
1833	Louis-Philippe opens the Museum of French History in Versailles.	
1870	Versailles becomes the Prussian headquarters during the Franco-Prussian War.	
1871	A peace treaty signed at Versailles ends the Franco-Prussian War. William I of Prussia is declared German Emperor in the Hall of Mirrors.	
1875	The Congressional Chamber is built in the South Wing.	

This painting illustrates the signing of the Treaty of Versailles in the Hall of Mirrors in 1919. The Treaty stipulated that Germany should surrender territory and pay compensation for provoking World War I.

THE TREATY

During the early 1900s, alliances between European states became strained as they challenged each other for control of overseas territories. Matters came to a head in 1914, when World War I began, as Austria-Hungary and Germany declared war on Serbia and France. Much of the fighting took place in eastern France and Belgium, where Germany confronted the Allies (France, Britain, USA). Hundreds of thousands of soldiers and civilians died. The war ended when an Armistice was agreed in November 1918. The following year, leaders of the Allies met at Versailles to negotiate a peace treaty. The Treaty of Versailles essentially blamed Germany for the war, and demanded heavy penalties. Germany had to hand over most of its overseas territories, it had to return Alsace-Lorraine to France and it had to pay war reparations. The Treaty of Trianon, between the Allies and Hungary, followed in 1920. The humiliation of the Versailles Treaty and the hardships caused by reparations contributed to the rise of the Nazi party in Germany, and to World War II (1939–45).

PEACEFUL TIMES

Charles de Gaulle, a former leader of the Resistance during World War II was elected president of the Fifth Republic in 1958. Under de Gaulle, Versailles once again resumed its place in French public life, when a wing of the Grand Trianon became a residence of the French head of state. Since then, Versailles has hosted many international heads of state, including leaders of the Soviet Union, Nikita Khrushchev, Leonid Brezhnev and Mikhail Gorbachev; Presidents of the USA, John F. Kennedy and Richard Nixon; and Queen Elizabeth II.

1919	The Treaty of Versailles establishes the peace settlement after the end of the World War I.
1966	The Trianon-sous-Bois becomes a residence of the French president.
1999	On December 26, 10,000 trees in the grounds of Versailles are uprooted by hurricane-force winds.

In this photograph, President John F. Kennedy (middle floor, fifth from left) attends a concert at Versailles alongside French President Charles de Gaulle.

CHAPTER 3

Exploring Versailles

Versailles is a big place. First there is the palace itself, with a string of rooms to visit. In the magnificent gardens and park, there are dozens of beautiful fountains and statues, plus two smaller palaces, the Grand Trianon and the Petit Trianon, and Marie Antoinette's mock country hamlet, the Hameau de la Reine. Outside the palace gates lie the historic tennis court, and the stables which house the carriage museum. Seeing everything takes at least a whole day, so it is wise to plan a visit carefully.

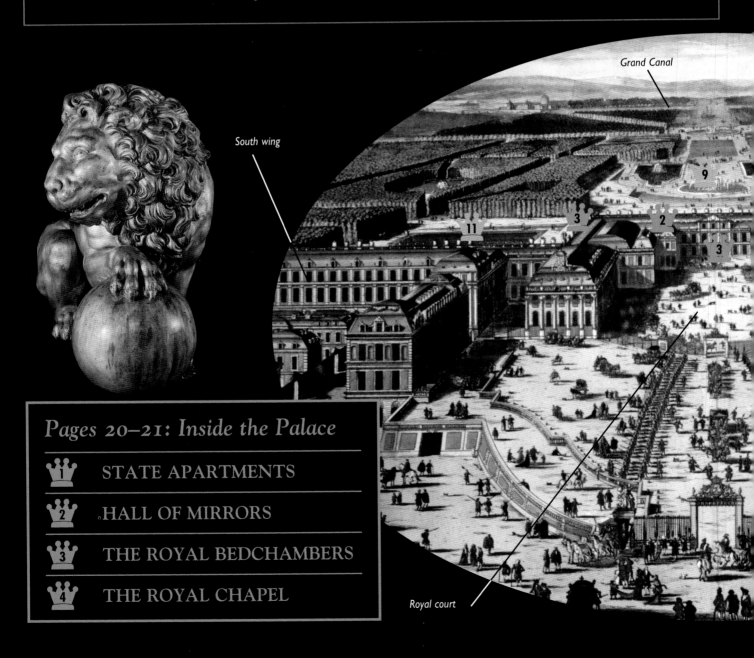

Grand Canal

South wing

Royal court

Pages 20–21: Inside the Palace

5 6 8
7

10

1

4

12*

North wing

* Carriage Museum, out of view

The Palace of Versailles

 ## STATE APARTMENTS

The seven STATE APARTMENTS were designed to impress visitors. The rooms are named after Roman gods and goddesses. The Salon of Hercules was specially designed by Robert de Cotte in 1710–30 to contain a painting by Veronese called *Christ at the House of Simon the Pharisee*. It remains the greatest work of art on display at Versailles. At the end of the series is the Salon of Apollo, which served as the throne room of the Sun King.

The Salon of Apollo from the Palace of Versailles' State Apartments is one of seven such ornately decorated rooms dedicated to Roman gods and goddesses.

The Hall of Mirrors is one of the palace's most popular rooms. Beautiful paintings adorn the ceiling and walls, while mirrors and chandeliers glisten.

THE HALL OF MIRRORS

Jules Hardouin Mansart's HALL OF MIRRORS has been considered one of the most famous rooms in Europe since it was completed in 1684. Originally solid silver furniture added to the glittering effect, but Louis XIV had to melt it down to help pay for his wars. The 17 mirrors are actually made up of 578 smaller panes. The ceiling depicts events in the first 17 years of Louis XIV's reign.

THE ROYAL BEDCHAMBERS

The reigning queen had a separate suite of rooms, facing south and overlooking the gardens. This was where she could hold court. The most magnificent room was the Queen's Bedchamber, to which only her closest courtiers were invited. It was also where the queen gave birth to her children, watched by an audience. The Queen's Bedchamber has been restored to how it would have looked at the time of Marie Antoinette. The king had another private suite of rooms overlooking the courtyards. They included the King's Bedchamber, at the very centre of the building. Luxuriously decorated, this is where Louis XIV began and ended his day. He actually slept in another room called the 'Petite Chambre du Roi'.

The rich gold and red brocade hangings in the Queen's Bedchamber have been restored to how they looked during Queen Marie Antoinette's reign.

THE ROYAL CHAPEL

Dedicated to St. Louis, the chapel was completed in 1710, towards the end of Louis XIV's reign. It is the tallest part of the palace, with an interior space soaring to 25 metres. The king, who attended Mass daily as part of his court ritual, would sit on the 'tribune' on the upper level, overlooking the courtiers below.

The Royal Chapel in the North Wing of the palace is dominated by grand neoclassical pillars and archways.

This carved lion detail is from a chair that was made in 1681 for the royal chapel at Versailles – a gift from Louis XIV.

The mirror salon from the left wing of the Grand Trianon has been decorated with furnishings from the 19th century.

GRAND TRIANON

The unique mixture of stone and pink marble that covers the exterior of the Grand Trianon was Louis XV's own idea. These days, part of the building, the Trianon-sous-Bois, is reserved for the use of the president of France. The interior of the Grand Trianon was originally decorated in luxurious style by Louis XIV and Louis XV, and then refurbished by Napoleon for his wife, Empress Marie-Louise, in 1810. The interior retains a mixture of all these styles.

Completed in 1768, the Petit Trianon was inhabited by many royal mistresses.

PETIT TRIANON

The Petit Trianon was built between 1763 and 1768, in the Greek style that was fashionable at the time. Louis XVI gave it to Marie Antoinette when he came to the throne in 1774, and she used it as a private mansion. The interior was redecorated by Empress Eugénie, wife of Napoleon III, in the 1860s, in the style of Louis XVI. The Petit Trianon dining room was created for Louis XV so he could eat his dinner among friends, away from public view. By an ingenious scheme, the tables could be lowered into the floor to the kitchen below, where they could then be recharged with food.

QUEEN'S HAMLET

The Queen's Hamlet was built in 1775–85 for Marie Antoinette as a place where she could play out her country fantasies – of a kind made popular by the poets and writers of the time. The lake-side buildings (some of which have disappeared) were designed to look like real farm dwellings, and included a mill and a dairy. But they also contained luxurious rooms for dining and entertaining.

The 'Queen's Cottage' in the Queen's Hamlet contained a billiards room and a series of elegantly decorated rooms for entertaining.

 ## TEMPLE OF LOVE

Marie Antoinette redesigned the gardens around the Petit Trianon, causing outrage by destroying Louis XV's famous botanical garden to create an English-style garden. Among the features that she introduced was a Greek-style 'Temple of Love', built in 1777–78.

The Temple of Love is located in the Petit Trianon gardens. With its twelve marble columns and domed roof, it is distinctly Greek in style.

The Palace of Versailles

This painting shows Louis XIV taking a walk with his entourage before the immaculately manicured formal gardens.

Carriage Museum, out of view

 THE FORMAL GARDENS

The garden nearest the palace is laid out on a set of descending terraces, divided neatly into geometric forms made up of pools and patterns of clipped box-hedges. (There are 21 kilometres of box-hedges in all). Designed by Le Nôtre, this is a classic example of a French-style formal garden.

 THE NEPTUNE FOUNTAIN

There are 32 ponds and 50 fountains at Versailles. Many of these are decorated with sculptures depicting Greek and Roman gods and mythical figures. A series of fountains was designed to tell the story of Apollo the Sun god rising in his chariot at dawn, and ending at the Grotto of Thetis with the nymphs who attended Apollo at dusk. One of the most spectacular fountains is the Bassin de Neptune, which has 58 spouts and produces 147 different effects.

The Neptune Fountain continues a running theme at Versailles of depicting Greek and Roman gods and goddesses.

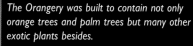

The Orangery was built to contain not only orange trees and palm trees but many other exotic plants besides.

 THE ORANGERY

Oranges were the height of luxury in Louis XIV's time. Beneath the terrace outside the South Wing is the Orangery, where hundreds of orange trees and palm trees were protected from the winter cold in their individual tubs. In the summer, the trees were – and still are – wheeled out and displayed on the terrace. The steps on either side are called the Great 100-Step Staircases. The Orangery also contains King Louis XIV's marble bathtub.

CARRIAGE MUSEUM

The two massive stables (the Grande Écurie and the Petite Écurie) outside the palace gates, on the Place d'Armes, were not just stables for 600 horses, but also barracks and accommodation blocks for grooms, pages and musicians. The Grande Écurie contains the Carriage Museum, with coaches collected by King Louis-Philippe. One of the oldest was used in the marriage of Napoleon to Marie-Louise in 1810.

The carriage museum is located in the building that once contained the royal stables and grooms' quarters.

CHAPTER 4

The people

Many of the great events in French history took place at Versailles and were also coloured by court intrigues and by the complex private lives of the French kings. The last 'King of the French', Louis-Philippe, may have abandoned the throne in 1848, but since that time Versailles has remained one of the nation's great palaces, and leaders on the world stage have continued to come through its doors.

Louis XIV ruled France for 72 years – a longer reign than any other major European monarch.

LOUIS XIV

Louis XIV was the first child of Louis XIII and Anne of Austria, after 22 years of marriage, so he was nicknamed Louis 'Dieudonné' ('Godgiven'). After the death of France's chief minister, Mazarin,

Louis XIV was deemed old enough to assume the throne – at which time he decided to take over complete control of government. Obsessed with detail, Louis was devoted to his duty as king, worked tirelessly and treated himself like public property that should always be on show to the nation. Believing himself to be second only to God, Louis was both kindly and ruthless. His weakness was flattery: his ministers, generals, courtiers and mistresses knew that they could get their way by telling him what he wanted to hear.

MARIE-THÉRÈSE OF AUSTRIA

The daughter of Philip IV of Spain, Marie-Thérèse was Louis XIV's cousin, and almost exactly the same age. Their marriage in 1660 was designed to heal the wounds of the Thirty Years War (1618–48), during which France had supported the Protestant

Marie-Thérèse, wife of Louis XIV, is shown here with her son Louis – otherwise known as 'The Grand Dauphin' – who died before his father.

powers against the Catholic Spain. It also brought together the Bourbon family of France with the Habsburgs of Spain and Austria. Louis had met Marie-Thérèse only three days before the wedding and he soon lost interest in her, at which time she had to learn to share her husband with his mistresses. She bore him six children; only one of whom

Louis XIV descended from Louis IX, also known as Saint Louis (reigned 1226–70), a crusader-king famed for his honesty, virtue and sense of justice. By tradition, Louis XIV inherited his miraculous healing powers, which were passed to him during the coronation ceremony. At Versailles, the sick would gather in the Stone Gallery each day, hoping that Louis XIV, in his procession to the Chapel, might touch them and cure them.

survived, a son called Louis, the 'Grand Dauphin' (Crown Prince), but he died four years before his father in 1711 and never became king of France. Marie-Thérèse died in 1683, a year after the royal court had moved to Versailles.

LOUIS XIV'S MISTRESSES

Louise de La Vallière was just 16 when she became the King's mistress in 1660. Rising from humble origins, and with a slight limp, she was a celebrated beauty. She was a centre of attention at the great festival at Versailles, called the 'Pleasures of the Enchanted Island' in 1664. She fell from favour when the king turned his attentions to Madame de Montespan, and retired to a convent. Madame de Montespan entered court as lady-in-waiting to Marie-Thérèse, and was mistress to Louis XIV from 1667 to 1679. A

vivacious beauty, she was the leading lady of Versailles for over a decade, a position she jealously guarded against all rivals to the King's attention.

Madame de Montespan's reputation was wrecked by her involvement in the Poison Scandal – which revealed that she

The French kings were famously public with their infidelities. Besides lavish gifts of the finest clothes and shoes (such as this delicately embroidered leather shoe from Louis XIV's reign) many French kings gave their mistresses their own accommodation.

This detail from the ceiling painting in the Hall of Mirrors documents France's renewed alliance with the Swiss against the Habsburgs.

had taken part in black-magic seances with various unsavoury characters in Paris.

Madame de Maintenon was governess to the children of Louis XIV and Madame de Montespan, and became mistress to Louis XIV from 1675 – especially after Madame de Montespan fell from favour. She married the king in a secret night-time ceremony in

October 1683, three months after the death of Queen Marie-Thérèse. She had a strong influence on Louis in the latter part of his life.

ARCHITECTS AND CRAFTSMEN

A leading French architect of his day, Louis Le Vau designed the château of Vaux-le-Vicomte for Nicolas Fouquet, before being recruited by Louis XIV to rebuild the Louvre in Paris. He masterminded the first two phases of rebuilding at Versailles. Also one of Fouquet's team, Charles Le Brun was appointed Chief Painter to the King, and took over the decoration of the main rooms of Versailles. One of his greatest works is the ceiling painting of the Hall of Mirrors.

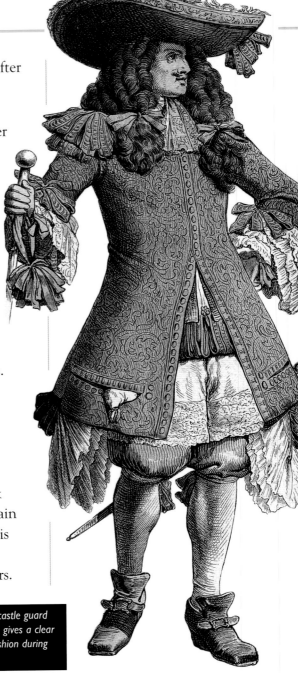

This Prussian engraving of officers of the castle guard during the era of Louis XIV (1638–1715) gives a clear indication of the importance placed on fashion during the period.

Tales & customs – ON THE THRONE

Almost every aspect of Louis XIV's life was on display – he would even receive guests when sitting on the lavatory. In fact, it was considered a great honour to be invited to do so. The kind of lavatory in question was a 'close stool' – a kind of chair with a hole in the seat and a potty underneath. The king's was particularly comfortable, decorated with Japanese scenes on black lacquer, and with a seat upholstered in velvet.

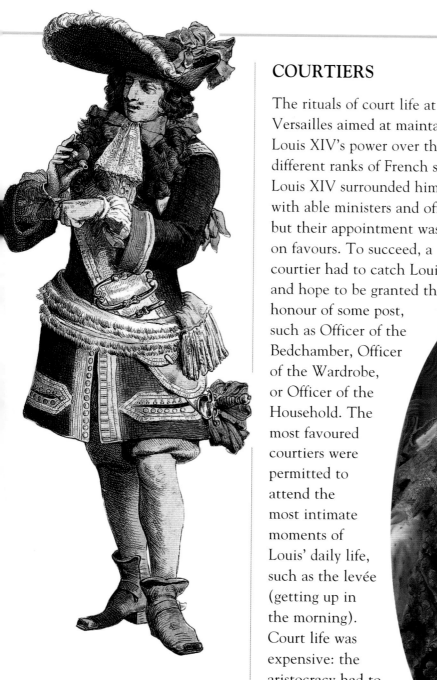

Botanist, architect and painter, the multi-talented André Le Nôtre was responsible for the gardens of Versailles. He became the royal gardener in 1673, a post that his father and grandfather had both held before him. Louis XIV was particularly fond of Le Nôtre. Le Nôtre, however, was extremely modest and refused any special honours.

COURTIERS

The rituals of court life at Versailles aimed at maintaining Louis XIV's power over the different ranks of French society. Louis XIV surrounded himself with able ministers and officials, but their appointment was based on favours. To succeed, a courtier had to catch Louis' eye and hope to be granted the honour of some post, such as Officer of the Bedchamber, Officer of the Wardrobe, or Officer of the Household. The most favoured courtiers were permitted to attend the most intimate moments of Louis' daily life, such as the levée (getting up in the morning). Court life was expensive: the aristocracy had to maintain households in Versailles, with staff, stables and carriages; they had to keep up with the latest fashions, and have plenty of money for gambling. The worst that could happen to a courtier was to fail to be noticed. Louis' most damning criticism about a courtier was 'I do not

Louis XV was King of France from 1723–1774. The Duc d'Orléans ruled on his behalf until Louis' 14th birthday.

know him'. Louis knew that, so with this combination of favouritism and expense, and his vast network of spies and informers, he could keep his court under control.

LOUIS XV

Louis XV (1710–74) was the successor to his great-grandfather Louis XIV – both his father and his grandfather had died – and so Louis came to the throne at the age of just five, and his reign lasted 59 years. In 1725, aged 15, he married Marie Leszczynska, daughter of the king of Poland. They had 10 children, but only seven survived. Louis XV was shy, and a far more private man than Louis XIV, and he spent much of his time in retreat from the court in his private apartments and at the Grand Trianon. Louis XV's reign was marred by the loss of many of France's overseas territories (in North America and India) during the Seven Years War, and by mounting debts that paved the way for the French Revolution. He died of smallpox at Versailles.

MADAME DE POMPADOUR

Madame de Pompadour was Louis XV's mistress from 1745 to 1750, but continued to play an important role at court and in politics after that date. She encouraged Louis to take part in the Seven Years War (1756–63), and so was blamed for the losses suffered by France. But at court she was welcomed for reviving intellectual debate and organising festivities, dinners and balls. She was a patron of the arts and to many writers and philosophers of the Enlightenment. She also

Madame de Pompadour was a colourful and flamboyant 18th century figure. Her life has continued to be celebrated, as in the operetta this 1933 poster is advertising.

had a great influence on tastes and fashion at court.

LOUIS XVI

The last of the great French kings to rule from Versailles was Louis XVI (1754–92). The grandson of Louis XV, he was generally popular, but suffered from indecision, and from being married to the deeply unpopular Marie Antoinette, who had a strong influence on his rule and choice of ministers. His reign was dominated by the growing financial crisis, which led to bankruptcy in 1788. His refusal to accept reform led to increasing hostility in the early days of the revolution. He lost all sympathy by encouraging

This lithograph from 1870 shows an aristocratic scene from King Louis XVI's day. Wealthy people spared no expense on the finest fashions. This displeased the common people who could barely afford food to feed their families.

Tales & customs – THE DIAMOND NECKLACE AFFAIR

This began when Comtesse de Lamotte persuaded a jeweller that she was buying a diamond necklace on Marie Antoinette's behalf. She tricked her lover, the Cardinal of France, into thinking he was writing to Marie Antoinette, and he took delivery of the necklace. The Comtesse gave it to her husband, who sold it in London. When the plot was discovered, Marie Antoinette insisted on taking the Cardinal to court. This was unwise, because it exposed her extravagant lifestyle and caused public indignation. The cardinal was acquitted.

opponents of the Revolution abroad, and attempting to flee to Austria in June 1791. His support for the counter-revolutionary war, launched by his Austrian nephew Francis II in 1792, led to his arrest for treason, and to his execution in 1793.

MARIE ANTOINETTE

The daughter of Maria Theresa and Francis I of Austria, Marie Antoinette (1755–93) married Louis XVI when she was 14 and he was 15. Young and arrogant, she made herself unpopular in the royal court through her favouritism and frivolity. She had little patience for the formal etiquette of Versailles, and made no effort to conceal her boredom. She preferred to retreat with her friends to the Petit Trianon and her fake rural farming village, the

This 19th century engraving shows Louis XVII, son of Louis XVI and Marie Antoinette. When his parents were taken to prison, the young Louis was subjected to the same fate. However, he mysteriously disappeared whilst there. Recent DNA tests on his supposed heart appear to support the claim that he died in prison, aged 10.

Hameau de la Reine. She was widely disliked by the French public. It was rumoured that, when she was told that the starving poor of Paris were rioting because they could not afford bread, she responded: 'Let them eat cake!' Accused of instigating Louis XVI to promote Austrian

resistance to the Revolution, she received little sympathy as she was taken for execution at the age of 37, in October 1793, in rags, in open cart, jeered by the crowd. However, in these final traumatic months, she behaved with remarkable courage and dignity.

THE 'LOST DAUPHIN' LOUIS XVII

The second son of Louis XVI and Marie Antoinette, Louis became Dauphin aged eight, just before the Revolution. In 1792 he was imprisoned with his family in Paris' Temple Prison. After the execution of his father, he was proclaimed king by royalists, but he probably died of tuberculosis in prison. Rumours suggested that he had escaped, giving rise to the legend of the 'Lost Dauphin' and a host of pretenders claiming to be the true heir to the throne of France.

NAPOLEON BONAPARTE

Napoleon Bonaparte (1769–1821) shot to fame as a dynamic young general during the Revolutionary Wars. In 1799, he took control of France as consul. He upheld many of the ideals of the Revolution, giving opportunities to talented people and introducing a modern set of laws. There was a brief spell of peace in 1802, then he resumed his military campaign, in an attempt to create a single European Empire, conquering Italy, Austria, Spain and Germany. But he met defeat at the hand of Nelson at the Battle of Trafalgar in 1805. Napoleon moved to Versailles after his marriage in 1810. He refurbished the Grand Trianon for his new bride, and he gave the Petit Trianon to his sister Pauline. Napoleon's campaign against Russia in 1812 was a disaster, and the French were defeated in 1814. Napoleon abdicated and was sent to the Italian island of Elba. He escaped in 1815, returned to France and raised an army, but was defeated at the Battle of Waterloo in June. He was sent to the remote island of Saint-Helena in the South Atlantic, where he died in 1821. Napoleon's second wife, Marie-Louise, was the

This detail from a painting shows the hand of Marie-Louise of Austria (Napoleon's second wife) – holding the imperial crown.

daughter of Francis II of Austria. She married Napoleon in 1810; she was 19 and he was 41. The marriage united the Austrian Empire with France. She refused to join Napoleon when he was first exiled to the Italian island of Elba, and in 1814 left Paris for Austria with their son. After Napoleon's death in 1821, she remarried and became Duchess of Parma, Italy.

KING LOUIS-PHILIPPE

A descendant of Philippe I, Duc d'Orléans (brother of Louis XIV), Louis-Philippe was chosen to become 'King of the French' when Charles X abdicated during the Revolution of 1830. Having supported the Revolution, he was considered by the middle classes to be one of them, and so was called 'the Bourgeois King'. He restored Versailles, and turned a wing of the palace into the Museum of French History, while he and his family lived in the Grand Trianon. He introduced reforms, but his refusal to extend the vote to the middle classes caused resentment. He was forced to abdicate during the Revolution of 1848, and retired to Surrey, England, where he supposedly called himself 'Mr Smith'.

Tales & customs – THE FIRST AIR PASSENGERS

On 19 September, 1783 – witnessed by Louis XVI, Marie Antoinette and about 130,000 spectators – the brothers Joseph and Étienne Montgolfier attempted the first manned hot-air balloon flight. When they launched the balloon, from the courtyard in front of the palace of Versailles, their three passengers were a duck, a cock and a sheep. The animals landed safely after eight minutes in the air and a flight of 3.2 kilometres.

France after D-Day, he was made leader of the French government. In 1958, he was called back as head of government. He presented a new constitution and became president from 1959. De Gaulle understood the symbolic role of Versailles, and adapted the Trianon-sous-Bois as a presidential palace. Unrest and the defeat of his proposals for reform led to his resignation in 1969.

Widely regarded as one of the greatest military figures in history, Napoleon Bonaparte emerged from the chaos of the French Revolution to lead France as Emperor from 1804 to 1814.

NAPOLEON III

A nephew of Napoleon I, Louis Bonaparte was elected president of the Second Republic in 1848, after the Revolution that had removed Louis-Philippe. In 1852, he took the title of Emperor, and ruled as Napoleon III until France lost the Franco-Prussian War in 1871. In 1853 he married Eugénie de Montijo, who renovated the Petit Trianon during the 1860s. Napoleon III also restored much of the gardens of Versailles.

CHARLES DE GAULLE

In 1940, during World War II, Germany invaded France. Charles de Gaulle, French Under-secretary of National Defence and War, fled to Britain to lead the French Resistance. Before the recapture of

Charles de Gaulle was the leader of the Free French Forces in World War II and in 1958, after a constitutional crisis, he became the first president of the Fifth Republic.

Versailles began as a pleasure palace, first as a lodge for hunting ('the sport of kings'), then as a scene for the representation of the powerful French monarchy. Throughout its history, Versailles has been the setting for plays, opera and music. Today, the palace has a busy schedule of exhibitions, concerts and performances, including spectacular summer shows combining music and fountains.

THE PLEASURES OF THE ENCHANTED ISLAND

Louis XIV held spectacular festivities at Versailles, even before the palace was completed. In 1664, just two years after work had begun on the gardens of Versailles, Louis XIV hosted one of the most spectacular parties in history. It was called 'The Pleasures of the Enchanted Island'. Queen Anne, the King's mother, was the guest of honour, but Louis was also celebrating his love for his young mistress, Louise de La Vallière. On the first night, the park was lit by torch-light and many thousands of candles. In an open-air theatre, Louis himself played the lead role in a play called *Orlando Furioso*, entering on horseback, followed by a procession of dozens of costumed performers, animals from the menagerie and the glittering chariot of Apollo. The play – about an enchanted island – was made magical through special effects, culminating in a huge fireworks display. The week continued with a jousting tournament by day and, by night, theatre, concerts, dances and ballet, and outdoor feasts served by staff dressed as fauns and wood-nymphs.

Many events at Versailles close with an awe-inspiring fireworks and light-show display as captured in the photograph above.

Tales & customs – FRENCH LITERATURE

The three great French dramatists – Molière, Corneille and Racine – all worked at Versailles for Louis XIV. Molière produced a wide range of court entertainment, but he is best known for his comedies, while Corneille and Racine wrote tragedies. Another famous author and poet closely involved with the Versailles of Louis XIV was La Fontaine, best known for his collections of animal fables.

This 17th century engraving shows a stage set for a theatre production at Versailles. Plays by the great French dramatists Molière, Corneille and Racine were performed on temporary stages at Versailles, at the bidding of Madame de Maintenon and Madame de Montespan.

LIVELY EVENINGS AT THE PALACE

Events were part of court life – a way of keeping the court loyal and entertained. Throughout the winter season, when the court was at Versailles, there was a daily programme of entertainment: plays by the leading dramatists of the time and music played by the three palace ensembles. Music, in fact, accompanied all events – in the State Apartments, in the gardens, during boating excursions on the Grand Canal and even during hunting trips.

Three times a week, an evening event took place in the State Apartments. The evening began at 6 pm with a concert. Then there was dancing, card-games, gambling, food and drink. The evenings ended at 10 pm, when the company went to watch the

This 1670 watercolour fan painting shows a boat-load of Louis XIV's guests at a fête on the grand canal.

royal family dine at the Grand Couvert, held in the Antechamber of the King's Suite.

SPECIAL OCCASIONS

Each year there were special occasions, such as the stately procession of the Knights of the Order of the Holy Spirit, held on 2 January, which ended in a ceremony in the Royal Chapel. Big occasions – such as royal weddings, celebrations of military victories, visits by foreign ambassadors – were celebrated in grand style. One of the most famous was the marriage for the future Louis XVI and Marie Antoinette in 1770, for which 6,000 invitations were issued – and some 200,000 members of the public turned up to witness the three-day spectacle. The Opera House was completed for the occasion, ingeniously constructed

35

so the auditorium floor could be raised to the stage level to create a spectacular dining room and ballroom; it could be lowered again for opera performances. The whole park was magically illuminated to create a kind of opera of light.

FOUNTAINS, MUSIC, FIREWORKS!

The tradition of festivity continues today with regular concerts held at the Opera House, the Royal Chapel and the Salon of Hercules. A series of special exhibitions is mounted each year in various apartments, galleries and halls, each celebrating some aspect of Versailles' history, and its cultural contribution to France and the world at large. But the most

The grand diva of rock, Tina Turner, performs on stage at Versailles. Many other contemporary performers have staged concerts at the palace.

famous special events take place in the gardens during summer, each specially designed to evoke the glorious days of royal Versailles. The 'Grand Musical Waters' is a tour of the fountains, accompanied by music of the 17th and 18th centuries. The tour takes visitors around the route that Louis XIV himself devised to see the best viewpoints over the gardens, which includes nine major fountains and 12 woodland groves. The finale takes place at the Neptune Fountain, where 99 water spouts shoot ten metres into the air, accompanied by the music of Handel.

Even more spectacular, however, are the 'Grand Nocturnal Waters', which take place on Saturday nights in July.

Beginning at sunset, visitors are taken on a magical musical tour of the garden and groves to see the fountains, all beautifully

Tale & customs – NO TIME FOR LUNCH

In June, 1791, Louis XVI and Marie Antoinette were given an opportunity to flee to safety in Austria. Dressed as servants, they fled under the cover of darkness. However, for comfort they took a large, slow carriage, and Louis insisted on stopping for a picnic, wasting crucial time. News of their escape travelled fast; at Varennes, 40 miles short of safety, they were recognised and taken back to Paris.

Lighting is often used to clever effect in combination with the dramatic fountain system during performances at Versailles, such as in this scene from an opera and light show from last decade.

even watch from boats floating on the fountain's huge pond. Each year the show has a different theme, connected with Versailles. In 2004, for instance, the show was based around the story of the Chevalier de Saint-George, a noble at the court of Marie Antoinette. He was unusual because his father was a plantation owner and his mother a black slave; he was born on the Caribbean island of Guadeloupe. The Chevalier de Saint-George was a celebrated musician, composer, swordsman and horseman, and the show combined all these elements. It was designed and choreographed by the famous horse-trainer and showman Bartabas, who used 50 Lusitanian horses now stationed at the Grande Écurie, along with a large team of percussionists, actors and dancers – and of course fireworks.

The Opera House built by King Louis XV at Versailles often hosts lavish balls and operas. A model poses above in a gown that befits the dramatic architecture.

illuminated. The music of Lully is prominently featured, because he wrote music especially to accompany Louis XIV's outdoor festivities. The music and settings unfold in a drama of four themes: music for nocturnal festivities music for sleep, the music of nightmares (evoking demons and witches), and lastly, music for prayer and reflection. Complementing the music are performances by costumed theatrical groups, musicians playing authentic instruments,

fire-eaters and palace guards in the uniforms of Louis XIV. The programme ends with a firework display – just as Louis XIV would have wished it.

THE BIG SUMMER SHOW

For more than 40 years now, Versailles has put on a spectacular outdoor late-summer show, at the end of August and beginning of September. Stands are erected beside the Neptune Fountain with enough seating for 50,000 people, and some of the audience can

CHAPTER 6

Uncovering the past

V ersailles is magnificent. But it is still just a shadow of what it once was. In the days of Louis XIV it astonished the world with its sumptuous luxury – filled with exquisite furniture, paintings, tapestries, books and vases. Above all, it was full of people, dressed in costumes of exceptional lavishness. Today, we need imagination to restore in our mind's eye the full impression of Versailles as it once was.

SOURCE MATERIAL

There is no shortage of documentation about the palace of Versailles. In the palace collection alone there are 6,000 paintings, 1,500 drawings and

This intricate design for the Queen's Theatre in the Petit Trianon was designed by the architect Richard Mique in 1786.

15,000 engravings. There are architects' drawings, paintings, engravings, maps and written descriptions that tell us how the palace was built and how it changed over time. There are

This photograph of the bedchamber of Marie Antoinette in the Queen's Apartments clearly conveys just how extravagant the Queen's tastes were.

public records, printed books, newspaper articles and private diaries that tell us what went on there. Bills show us what items were purchased, and how much was spent. All these give us insight into the history of Versailles.

PALACE OF AN ABSOLUTE MONARCH

Louis XIV wanted to created the biggest, most impressive palace in Europe – the palace that all other kings would try to copy, the palace that would leave visitors gasping with astonishment. That was its history from 1661 to 1789. But we can also look at Versailles and see how it was a symbol of extravagance and waste. While the royal family and nobles frittered away their time and money at Versailles, the middle classes had to pay heavy taxes, and the poor barely had enough to eat. The grand rooms of Versailles may be splendid, but they are also

Amidst uncertainty about the future purpose of Versailles, King Louis-Philippe turned the palace into a Museum of French History.

echoing, empty rooms. An obvious target for the revolutionaries of 1789, Versailles remained a rather awkward reminder of the past swept aside by the Revolution. Yet it was too grand, too famous, too much of an achievement to demolish. After the Revolutions of 1830, King Louis-Philippe tried to resolve this awkwardness by making Versailles into a Museum of French History. It has since become a National Palace, with its Congress Hall for parliamentary sessions, and with official functions in the State Apartments.

THE TREASURE HUNT

The French authorities have decided to do whatever is possible to recreate how Versailles looked when it was in its full glory. One way of doing this is to bring back to it as many original items of furniture and other objects a possible. In 1962, a government

---

Tales & customs – BUT WHAT'S IT WORTH?

The best pieces of furniture in Versailles did not come cheap. The most expensive item bought by Louis XV was a roll-top desk (a prototype for all roll-top desks), made by one of the leading furniture makers of the day. It cost 65,000 livres, which in today's money would be about UK£120,000. All the furniture of Versailles was sold during the Revolution of 1793, and while a few pieces have since been recovered, most remain in private hands.

decree ordered that all objects from Versailles in French museums should be restored to the palace. Unfortunately, many of the most valuable items are not in French museums. After an auction of 1792, some were sold to private individuals; and many of them went abroad. The Sèvres porcelain of Louis XVI and Marie Antoinette, for instance, is now in the British royal collection. Experts have been keeping a close eye on auction rooms around the world; furniture from Versailles has been bought in sales in the USA, London and Tokyo.

UNDER THE MAGNIFYING GLASS

With their wealth and power, Louis XIV, XV and XVI could afford to employ the best craftsmen in the world. Their furniture is made of beautiful foreign woods, decorated with gold and semi-precious stones, all shaped and carved and polished to perfection. Their clocks represented not only the finest craftsmanship, but the leading edge of science and technology of their day. The porcelain plates from which they ate were produced to a standard that has never really been matched, even today. Their clothes were made of the finest and most expensive cloth, which was then tailored,

lined and embroidered to the most exquisite standards.

Each of these priceless items represents many hundreds of hours

This distinctive porcelain plate from 1823 has a painted scene from the period of Louis XVI. It was made at the royal porcelain factory at Sèvres.

of work. Versailles was at the tip of a complex system of trade, involving craftworkers, shopkeepers and merchants, down to the labourer cutting flax required to make linen. The complexity of this world can be detected in many of the objects now on view at Versailles.

THE FINEST GARB

An interesting example is the portrait of Louis XIV, by Hyacinthe Rigaud. Here he is seen standing before his throne, looking very grand and mighty, aged 62 and in full regalia. He is

wearing full court dress, with lace ruff and cuffs, silk breeches and silk stockings with garters, and high-heeled shoes with diamond-studded buckles. His ermine-lined mantle is in royal blue, embroidered with the fleur-de-lys (lily), the symbol for the French royal family. Also depicted are the symbols of his kingship: the crown; the sword of Charlemagne (the 8th century King of the Franks and later Roman Emperor), representing his role as protector of the Church and the kingdom; and the sceptre, the ancient symbol of royalty.

THE KINGS' PASSIONS

Louis XV was fascinated by science, technology and craftwork, and would even make his own ironwork; he carved ivory and experimented with cookery. Perhaps the most extraordinary evidence of this interest can be seen in the astronomical clock (in the Clock Cabinet of the apartments of Louis XV). It can show the time, the phases of the Moon, the movement of the planets, and the date until the year 9999. Completed in 1754, it took a clockmaker and an engineer 12 years to make.

Like many noblemen of the time, Louis XVI was an avid collector of things that interested him. This is

Tales & customs – GHOSTLY APPARITIONS?

In 1901, two English women had a strange experience near the Petit Trianon. They came to a cottage beside a gazebo where they saw a man in 18th-century costume with a heavily pock-marked face and a woman in old-fashioned dress sitting and sketching. Later, they discovered that the cottage, gazebo and bridge had all existed in 1789, but not in 1901. Also, the woman had looked just like a painting of Marie Antoinette.

Louis XIV surrounded himself with finery. From the rich fabrics of his robes to the fine foreign woods of his furniture. This painting by Hyacinthe Rigaud captures something of the King's love of material things.

This beautiful cabinet of Louis XVI is decorated with insects and plants made from real feathers and insect wings, and finished with gold inlay.

perhaps best illustrated in a cabinet that he had made to store gold coins in 1788 (now in Louis XV's apartments at Versailles). The surfaces of the cabinet are decorated with birds, butterflies and plants, all made from feathers and beetles' wings. Such objects give us glimpses into the character of the kings who ruled Versailles, and the way a powerful monarchy represented itself.

CHAPTER 7

A day in the life

About nine million people visit Versailles every year, two-thirds of whom are foreigners. Of these, 3 million tour the house, and 6 million visit the grounds. In other words, Versailles is one of the top visitor attractions in France. Looking after Versailles, and all its visitors is therefore a major undertaking. And the best advice to any visitor, especially in the busy summer season is: get there early!

Drivers of horse-drawn carriages, who offer rides to visitors in the park, are just some of the many people who make a living by working at Versailles.

RUNNING VERSAILLES

Up to 800 people are employed to look after Versailles. This includes 363 guards, who patrol the rooms and the grounds; 48 gardeners; 11 curators, who look after and maintain the palaces and their precious contents, and who also carry out historical research; three architects who are specialists in the conservation of historic buildings; 18 art restorers; 40 lecturers and guides and eight fountain technicians. In addition, there are cleaners, carpenters, plumbers and staff running the restaurants and shops, the boat-hire, mini-train and horse-drawn carriages. Versailles belongs to the French nation. It is therefore run as a public institution, like any of the major national galleries and museums. But for ten years now the palace has had its own administrative organisation that works to preserve and improve the famous site.

Today, the 48 gardeners at Versailles are constantly occupied with tending the extensive gardens at the palace.

OPEN TO THE PUBLIC

The Palace of Versailles is closed on Mondays and certain French public holidays, but is otherwise open every day of the year. Many local people treat the park of Versailles as a public space. Access is free, but visitors must buy a ticket for the formal gardens next to the palace. Both are open for far longer hours than the palace, virtually from dawn to dusk.

It is possible to visit Versailles as a day trip from Paris, but it is a good idea to set out early as there is so much to see. Only half of the treasures of Versailles are on display to the public. The rest are in safe-keeping.

THE GUIDES AT VERSAILLES

The tour guides at Versailles are incredibly knowledgeable about Versailles' past, cleverly weaving the history in with references to what you can see before you. They also keep their audiences entertained with anecdotes and stories, such as the one associated with a painting that clearly illustrates Napoleon's contempt for the Church. Napoleon invited Pope Pius VII to his coronation, where he was to be crowned the Emperor of France. However, when the Pope went to place the crown on the new king's head, Napoleon snatched the crown from his hands and placed it upon his own head. This showed that Napoleon believed that the Pope had no legitimate right to crown him because in the 'new France' the Church had no power over the State.

A typical day at Versailles – visitors stroll near the Fountain of Latona, the mother of Apollo. A complete trip on foot around the gardens and park can take hours.

Myths and legends – THE DAILY SPECTACLE

Virtually every aspect in King Louis XIV's life was a public performance and his court was obsessive about ceremony and ritual. Each day was planned to the last minute and detail, from waking to going to bed at night. This rigorous and jealously guarded order of things was attended by select courtiers chosen according to whoever the king favoured at any particular time.

CHAPTER 8

Preserving the past

The conservation team at Versailles is constantly busy maintaining and preserving the palace buildings, furnishings and gardens. As well as this continuing work, some major incidents have damaged the palace complex and caused extra work. These include a bomb explosion in 1978, and a hurricane in 1999 that toppled about 10,000 trees.

Restoration work at Versailles is ongoing. Any such work is carefully directed by art historians and archaeologists. About 20 years ago, more than 80 rooms were renovated, funded by the French government. This permitted the ground-floor apartments of the Dauphin and Dauphine to be opened to the public.

TIME AND NATURE

With three million visitors passing through the palace every year, and the threat of damage by weather and insects, keeping Versailles in good condition is a constant challenge. This is the daily task of Versailles' team of 18 art restorers, and there are many factors they must take into account. When the Treaty of Versailles was signed in 1919, the palace and the park were in a dilapidated state. In the 1920s, with the assistance of grants from the American oil-tycoon John D. Rockefeller Jr, modern restoration began, and has continued ever since. Two magnificent projects have set high standards for restoration at the palace. The Queen's Bedchamber was restored in 1975 to the sumptuous style of Marie Antoinette, and the King's Bedchamber was restored in 1980. The real triumphs here were the restoration of the beds and their elaborate hangings, which give some indication of the richness of cloth and textiles that surrounded the royal court in the 17th and 18th centuries.

The extraordinary Fountain of Enceladus – depicting a mythical

The King's Bedchamber was renovated in 1980 to look exactly as it did while Louis XIV was King of France.

giant struggling under a pile of stones – was renovated and re-gilded in 1998, along with more rooms of the apartments of the Dauphin and Dauphine. The main project that historians are focusing on at present is the restoration of the Hall of Mirrors, starting with the floor, before moving on to the carved and painted wall decorations.

DISASTER STRIKES

Renovations became more pressing after several disasters took place at the palace in the 20th century. These include a bomb explosion inside the palace on 26 June, 1978 which caused widespread damage. The bomb had been placed there by activists demanding independence for Brittany. They targeted Versailles because they believed it was a symbol of French oppression. Then, in 1999, hurricane-force winds knocked down about 10,000 trees in the park of Versailles. These two events caused major setbacks for the team of conservationists at the palace.

The photograph above shows one of the many felled trees caused by the hurricane of December 1999.

Tales & customs – THE ROYAL GRILLE

The inner courtyard of the palace was originally protected by a golden fence and gate, which kept the public away from the courtyard beneath the windows of the royal apartments. Known as the 'Royal Grille' it was torn down during the Revolution. Under the current restoration programme, the plan is to reinstate it. This is a controversial project, as the equestrian statue of Louis XIV will have to be moved to make room for it.

Glossary

Abdicate Give up the role of king or queen to make way for a new monarch or different form of government to take the throne.

Absolute Power Power held completely by the king or queen. That is, the power is not shared with anyone else. The monarch rules entirely alone.

Apollo Ancient Roman and Greek God of the Sun – also traditionally associated with music and poetry. Louis XIV was often compared to Apollo. This is one reason why he was called the 'Sun King'.

Aqueducts Long bridge-type structures that hold and carry water to towns and cities.

Aristocracy Highest-ranking social class, including people with hereditary titles, such as: duke, marquis, earl, viscount, baron, knight and esquire.

Armistice A temporary war-time truce or peace ruled by agreement between the opposing sides.

Bankrupt Legally proven to lack the money to pay debts.

Château The French word for a large French country house or castle.

Civil war War that divides different factions within one state or country.

Coronation The ceremony where a new king or queen is officially crowned.

Courtiers Attendants or advisors to the king or queen who are in attendance at the royal court.

Dauphin The eldest son of the King of France (or Crown Prince).

D-Day The day during World War II (June 6, 1944) when the Allied Forces invaded Normandy in Northern France to attack German troops stationed there.

Declaration of Independence The declaration of the Congress of the 13 United States of America, on July 4, 1776, by which they formally declared that these colonies were free and independent states, not subject to the government of Great Britain.

Dictator A ruler who has total and tyrannical control of a country. The most well-known dictators were Hitler and Stalin.

Divine Right of Kings A theory which argued that certain kings were chosen by god to rule and that they were answerable to no-one but God.

Edict of Nantes Issued on April 13, 1598 by Henry IV of France, the Edict was a law that granted French Protestants (also known as Huguenots) rights and freedoms in a predominantly Catholic country.

Empire Large group of states ruled over by a single monarch or state.

Empire style Neoclassical style of clothing, architecture and the decorative arts that developed in France in the early 19th century during Napoleon Bonaparte's rule. It was meant to visually reflect the harmony of all things under Napoleon's leadership.

Enlightenment Intellectual and philosophical movement that developed in Europe during the 18th century that emphasised the use of reason to make sense of things.

Extravagant Going above and beyond what is necessary, for the sake of fashion or whim.

Façade The front face of a building.

French Revolution (1789–99) The overthrow of the French monarchy by the people of France who revolted against the extravagance of the monarchy. This marked the end of the French royal lineage of the Bourbons and the emergence of democracy and the right of the common people.

Grand Trianon A palace built in 1687 by Louis XIV for his mistress, Madame de Maintenon. It was originally called the Trianon de Marbre. Trianon was the name of the town cleared to make way for the first Trianon palace to be built (the 'Trianon de Porcelaine').

Huguenots French Protestants who were increasingly persecuted, particularly in the 16th and 17th centuries, until the French Revolution.

Menagerie Collection of wild animals kept in captivity for public entertainment. The menagerie at Versailles was established by Louis Le Vau at the request of Louis XIV.

Monarchy State or country in which supreme power is held by a monarch (king or queen).

Napoleonic Wars Series of French campaigns led by Napoleon Bonaparte against Austria, Russia, Great Britain and other European countries.

Neoclassical An art and architectural style that was strongly influenced by the art and architecture of Classical Greece and Rome.

Nobility The privileged social class. Another word for 'aristocracy'.

Parlements 13 regional royal courts in 18th century France that were empowered to register royal decrees before they became law. In this capacity, the parlements opposed royal initiatives that they believed threatened the freedom of the people.

Petit Trianon The mini-palace built by Louis XV for his mistress, Madame de Pompadour (see also Grand Trianon).

Philosophes A group of intellectuals who led the French Enlightenment and influenced the ideas of the French Revolution.

Prussia Former German state that covered what are now the central and eastern parts of Germany, the northern parts of Poland and a western province of Russia.

Regent A person who rules a state on behalf of a monarch who is too young to rule in his or her own right.

Reign of Terror A period during the French Revolution (1793–94) in which popular government carried out many executions of presumed enemies of the state.

Reparations Compensation for war damage paid by the defeated state.

Republic A state ruled by the people rather than a monarch.

Seance Meeting which can be of an esoteric or spiritual nature but can also mean a meeting of a club or a parliament.

Successor A person who takes over something from another person, such as a new king taking over from the old king.

Sun King King Louis XIV was known as the Sun King because of the success of his reign and magnificence of his court.

Third Republic Republican government that ruled France following the collapse of the Empire of Napoleon III in 1870.

Treason The crime of betraying one's country.

Treaty A legally-binding agreement between countries or states.

Tribune A raised platform on which a speaker stands to address a gathering.

Index

Copyright © ticktock Entertainment Ltd 2005
First published in Great Britain in 2005 by ticktock Media Ltd.,
Unit 2, Orchard Business Centre, North Farm Road, Tunbridge Wells, Kent, TN2 3XF
We would like to thank: Alison Howard, Susan Barraclough, Elizabeth Wiggans and Jenni Rainford for their help with this book.
Printed in China. A CIP catalogue record for this book is available from the British Library.

Picture Credits
AA World Travel Library: 1, 2–3, 19B, 24BL, 24B, Alamy: 4–5; Art Archive: 4B, 5T, 6R, 7, 8L, 8–9, 9B, 10L, 10–11, 11R, 12–13, 13T, 13B, 14, 14–15, 17T, 18T, 18–19, 19T, 20BL, 20–21, 21BL, 21TR, 21BR, 22T, 22B, 24–5, 25TR, 26R, 28, 28–9, 30T, 30–31, 32, 33L, 35T, 35B, 38L, 38R, 39R, 40, 41L; Bridgeman Art Library: 15T, 23B, 26L, 29R, 31T, 45T; Corbis: 6L, 17B, 23T, 27, 33R, 34, 36, 36–7, 37B, 42, 43L, 43R, 44–5, 45B